# God's Love Poured Out

*Living in The Overflow of God's Love*

Darlene Palmer

# God's Love Poured Out

*Living in The Overflow of God's Love*

Darlene Palmer

Copyright © 2020 by Darlene Palmer. All rights reserved.

This book or any portion thereof may not be reproduced or used in any manner whatsoever without the express written permission of the publisher or author except for the use of brief quotations in a book review.

Unless otherwise noted, scriptures marked KJV are taken from the KING JAMES VERSION (KJV): KING JAMES VERSION, public domain.

THE HOLY BIBLE, NEW INTERNATIONAL VERSION® NIV®

Copyright © 1973, 1978, 1984 by International Bible Society®

Used by permission. All rights reserved worldwide.

*"Scripture taken from the New King James Version®. Copyright © 1982 by Thomas Nelson, Inc. Used by permission. All rights reserved."*

*"Scripture quotations marked (NLT) are taken from the Holy Bible, New Living Translation, copyright © 1996, 2004, 2007 by Tyndale House Foundation. Used by permission of Tyndale House Publishers, Inc., Carol Stream, IL 60188. All rights reserved."*

Printed in the United States of America

First Printing, 2020

ISBN: 978-1-951883-34-8

Editor: G.E.M.

Interior Layout: Iris M. Williams

Design: Timilehin F. Olaitan

Palmer's Notepad Publishing

Moreno Valley, CA 92553

# DEDICATION

This devotional/journal is dedicated to my late husband, Elzie Lee Palmer Jr. He was a humble yet proud man who would always use his full name in referring to himself. I acknowledge his faithful love for the Lord which allowed him to extend unwavering support and unconditional love to me and our children. I am grateful for his thirty-two years of hard work providing for his family and allowing me to pursue my quest for knowledge and run after the extreme love of Christ. For this I am forever grateful.

I also dedicate this body of work to four magnificent children: Bryan, Tamara, Crystal, and Angela. They and their father hung with me as I transitioned in my Christian walk from faith to faith. They remained steadfast and unmovable through the many challenges, the ups and downs, and the joys and sorrows of family life.

I applaud each of them for their individual contributions to this devotional/journal by way of their unfailing love and dedication to my life's work and the various aspects of ministry. My heart is captured by their unconditional love towards one who is in pursuit of the extreme love of God.

*Blessed are the pure in heart: for they shall see God*
*(Matthew 5:8)*

Matthew 5:8, Blessed are the pure in heart: for they shall see God is the hallmark scripture for my life. I want to see God in all of His splendor and glory. The Bible assures us that this will happen when we all get to heaven; however, if possible, I want to get a glimpse of Him while I am here on earth. Moses, positioned in the cleft of a rock covered by God's hand, was given a glimpse of the backside of His glory, so we know it is possible. Perhaps my glimpse will come by way of His Word unfolding in my life and the lives of those around me.

Thus, my pursuit to see Him started with an exploration of His Word in hopes of gaining a portrait of His character. To my delight, the more I interact with His Word, the more I see Him. In every situation and trial of life, in all that is good and in all that is troublesome, I am able to capture a small glimpse of Him. I see His heart as He navigates my day to day life. I can see the strength and the fierceness of His protection and the extension of His compassionate arms reaching out to me. I can see His mercy, forgiveness, and the cleansing afforded me in my quest to become "pure in heart."

# TABLE OF CONTENTS

| | |
|---|---|
| Introduction | v |
| Help, A Misconception | 1 |
| Anchored | 5 |
| At the Crossroads | 9 |
| Behind the Scenes | 13 |
| Warning - Pay Close Attention | 17 |
| God's Love Comforts the Sorrowful | 21 |
| God's Love Covers Our Sin | 25 |
| God's Love Delivers | 29 |
| God's Love Discerns | 33 |
| God's Love is Everlasting | 37 |
| God's Love Gathers | 41 |
| God's Love is Gentle | 45 |
| God's Love Gives | 49 |
| God's Love Understands | 53 |
| God's Love Heals | 57 |
| God's Love Hears Our Cries | 61 |
| He's in There! | 65 |
| I AM A WINNER! | 69 |
| In His Time | 73 |
| God's Love Infused | 77 |
| God's Love Intercedes | 81 |
| Life Interrupted | 85 |

| | |
|---|---|
| God's Love Manifested | 89 |
| God's Love is Patient | 93 |
| God's Love Produces Fruit | 97 |
| God's Love Provides | 101 |
| God's Love is Reciprocal | 105 |
| God's Love Seeks True Worshippers | 109 |
| God's Love Restores Life | 113 |
| God's Love Unifies | 117 |
| God's Love Satisfies the Thirsty | 121 |
| God's Love Searches | 125 |
| Surrender | 129 |
| The Game Changer | 133 |
| The Real Enemy | 137 |
| God's Love Thinks Higher | 141 |
| God's Love is Truth | 145 |
| God's Love Laughs | 149 |
| God's Love is Watchful | 153 |
| What Shall I Do? | 157 |
| You Are the One | 161 |
| Your Choice | 165 |
| About the Author | 169 |

# FOREWORD

*My life journey is inspired by this Bible scripture, He found him in a desert land, and in the waste howling wilderness; he led him about, he instructed him, he kept him as the apple of his eye (Deuteronomy 32:10).*

I found the Lord in the midst of the waste howling wilderness where there appeared to be no means of escape. Hurt and rejection were my companions as a young adult as I navigated through years of an abusive marriage while trying to find some sense of normalcy. Without Christ in my life, I was lost and invisible.

To God, I was not lost; He could see me and knew exactly where I was. I could not see Him, nor would I have recognized Him through my veil of disappointment. Over the years, He sent many to show me the way and to help me see Him, but my eyes were blind, and my heart hardened. One day in desperation, I began reading a small pocket Bible that I found at the bottom of a drawer. Not knowing what to read, I found the table of contents with headings like "If you are afraid, read this," and "If you are lonely, read this," and "If you are hurting read this," etc. Reading what I assumed to be random scriptures started my journey in seeking the Lord.

In like manner, this book may appear to you as random scriptures but be assured every page is significant. Simply stated, this devotional/journal, filled with scripture is designed to speak to the individual heart. Its purpose is to challenge readers to look at and interact with their particular issues and emotions. The application and the takeaway are different for each individual as the events of our lives have taken different paths. But in the end, all paths ultimately lead us to the extreme love of God, as did my initial introduction to His love while searching the scriptures in the wilderness years of my life.

Today, I stand in a large place with my feet planted solidly upon the rock of Christ. I've been rescued from the waste howling wilderness by the gracious hand of a loving Father who keeps me as the apple of His eye. I cherish and am blessed by every opportunity given me to share the good news of the gospel and to help others experience God's extreme love that overflows into every aspect of life.

*Darlene Palmer*

# ACKNOWLEDGMENTS

I acknowledge the trials, tribulations, and the situations that boxed me in, backed me into corners over the course of my life, and contributed to my desperate pursuit for the extreme love of God.

I acknowledge all the people who are too numerous to count and the multitudes of those whom I have never met but had a part to play in the trials and tribulations, the ups and downs, the sorrows and disappointments, and the joys and the extreme pleasures of me coming to know Christ and His love. I salute you all.

# INTRODUCTION

This book is a compilation of experiences and interactions with Christ as the written Word. Each selection is a part of my life's journey to capture a glimpse of the Savior and to experience His heart of extreme love.

This journey took me beyond reading to the place of experience where the Word of God became a practical tool for living in the everyday world. The teachings, when applied, became my guideposts for successful living. The love of God manifested in countless ways not only intrigued me but has set the course for my life.

My prayer is for each reader to set aside the time it takes to catch a glimpse of Him in every selection. Page one, He may be a physician healing the sick and mending broken hearts, page fifteen, He may be an attorney representing you in the courts of heaven, then on page nineteen, He is an armor-clad warrior defeating the enemies of our soul. However presented, Christ can be found on every page.

This combination devotional journal is interactive and allows readers to incorporate themselves into each page by meditating on the thought-provoking and challenging questions. Feelings, emotions, and hidden thoughts will be stirred up and brought to the surface during reading. The healer, the deliverer, the joy giver, the peacemaker, the comforter desires to introduce and present Himself to you. This introduction opens the way for you to experience the love of God in every facet of your life.

My hope is that you will apply God's Word to your life. Therefore, I encourage you to read, meditate, journal your thoughts (as of the reading) and then revisit the questions six months from now and journal again.

# HELP, A MISCONCEPTION

*Give us help from trouble: for vain is the help of man*
*(Psalm 108:12).*

Help, an extension of God's love, can be expressed in countless ways. It is a small word with a multitude of meanings and applications: assistance, aid in accomplishing, rescue, support, rally around, bring a solution, comfort, ease, and so many more. Unfortunately, the word help in the Bible is misunderstood by most. It is often connected with the phrase, "God helps those who help themselves," which originated from ancient Greece and became popular in the modern world when it appeared in a version of "Poor Richard's Almanac." Since then, society has embraced it literally to mean that God helps only those who assist, alleviate, comfort, and somehow support themselves. This motto of self-help is often mistaken as a scriptural principle quote.

Hundreds of scriptures on help are quoted throughout the Bible like, *God is our refuge and strength, a very present help in trouble (Psalm 46:1); God is in the midst of her; she shall not be moved: God shall help her, and that right early (Psalm 46:5); and Having therefore obtained help of God, I continue unto this day (Acts 26:22).* God's offer of help is available for all who call upon His name, *For, whosoever shall call upon the name of the Lord shall be saved* (Romans 10:13).

Looking at Romans 10:13, it is clear that the responsibility is upon the individual person to make the initial call. This is where self-help comes into play. We help ourselves by calling upon His name. Too often, we try to handle problems and situations first, only calling on Him when we reach a blocked wall or a dead end. Calling upon His name must be our priority; it should be second nature for the Christian. The Lord desires to help His children and delights in those who trust and depend upon Him. Let us, therefore, put an end to the misconception that God helps only those who help themselves. He helps all those who call upon His name.

*He shall call upon me, and I will answer him (Psalm 91:15); call upon me in the day of trouble: I will deliver thee (Psalm 50:15);* and *I called upon the* Lord *in distress: the* Lord *answered me (Psalm 118:5).* These promises and more are for all those who call upon Him. The call can be made at any time of the day or night.

*Evening, and morning, and at noon, will I pray, and cry aloud: and he shall hear my voice (Psalm 55:17).*

**Reflect on the following and then use the space provided to journal your thoughts.**

- *Locate yourself in the reading. What thoughts and feelings immediately come to mind?*
- *Did the passage of scripture help or challenge you in any way?*
- *Were you able to recognize the extension of God's love in this reading?*
- *What do you take away from the reading? How will you apply what you've read?*
- *What will you share with others?*

# A Place for Your Thoughts (Now ...)
## A Misconception

Date: _____

# A Place for Your Thoughts (Sometime later ...)
## A Misconception

Date:

# ANCHORED

*Fear before him, all the earth: the world also shall be stable, that it be not moved (1 Chronicles 16:30).*

God's love is our stabilizing power. He made the world and set it upon an axis which has not moved or shifted since its inception. The orbit of the sun and the moon, the rotation of the earth, and the seas and the towering majestic mountains remaining in their places are all evidence of His power. In that, we must rejoice.

In the same way, the love of God stabilizes our individual lives. We are all subject to the winds of change, tragedies of death, and decisions of people which affect us in a multitude of ways. God's love is the grounding force that keeps us from being *tossed to and fro, and carried about with every wind of doctrine, by the sleight of men, and cunning craftiness, whereby they lie in wait to deceive (Ephesians 4:14).*

Consider the huge ships laden with people and cargo as they glide across the ocean's surface headed towards the dock. Once docked, they drop anchor to stabilize the ship, which has the buoyancy to stay afloat and the flexibility to roll with the waves of outgoing currents. We, too, must drop our anchor in the Lord and become stabilized. Then, we will have the buoyancy to stay afloat in turbulent and troubled waters that plague our lives. We must have the flexibility to roll with the waves thrown at us. Our ability to remain on top of the water depends on how deep our faith is anchored in Christ and His covenant promises. He never promised us smooth sailing, but He did promise that we could find hope and stability in Him.

True stability can only be found in Christ. He is the same today as He was yesterday, and as He will be tomorrow (Hebrews 13:8). The more we spend time in His presence and learn of Him, the deeper our anchor rests in Christ.

*But if the storms don't cease, and if the wind keeps on blowing, my soul has been anchored in the Lord.*
*~Douglas Miller*

**Reflect on the following and then use the space provided to journal your thoughts.**

- *Locate yourself in the reading. What thoughts and feelings immediately come to mind?*
- *Did the passage of scripture help or challenge you in any way?*
- *Were you able to recognize the extension of God's love in this reading?*
- *What do you take away from the reading? How will you apply what you've read?*
- *What will you share with others?*

# A Place for Your Thoughts (Now ...)
## Anchored

Date: _____

# A Place for Your Thoughts (Sometime later ...)
## Anchored

Date:

# AT THE CROSSROADS

*Behold, I will do a new thing; now it shall spring forth; shall ye not know it? I will even make a way in the wilderness, and rivers in the desert (Isaiah 43:19).*

At some point, we all stand at the crossroads having to choose which way to go and which direction to take. It is common to lean towards the familiar road which has been traveled many times. Repeated use has made the way comfortable, the road smooth, and has created the ability to navigate it without assistance. On the contrary, the unfamiliar road looks dark, strange, and uncertain, with the pavement uneven and winding. Assistance is required to journey on this road.

*Decision Time*

Everything says to take the familiar road where the visibility is clear, the pavement cracks are familiar, and you can navigate on your own. However, curiosity and the desire for something new is gnawing at you. Do you go with the familiar or step into unknown territory? The familiar should be the obvious road of choice considering the known facts, the time factor, and the ability to navigate independently. However, everything in you wants to escape the insanity of doing the same thing over and over again and expecting different results.

It's time to trust and take comfort in the love of the Lord, who is leading and guiding you into new things. It's time to heed the Lord's calling, *Behold, I will do a new thing, now it shall spring forth; Shall you not know it? I will even make a road in the wilderness and rivers in the desert (Isaiah 43:19).* It's time to trust Him in the unknown, *For I know the plans I have for you… plans to prosper you and not to harm you, plans to give you hope and a future (Jeremiah 29:11 NIV).*

Choosing to trust God may lead you down an unfamiliar and often uncomfortable road, yet it is all a part of His plan for your life. Mary, the mother of Jesus, stepped into the unfamiliar when she made the statement, *Behold the handmaid of the Lord; be it unto me according to thy word (Luke 1:38).* Mary's decision to follow the Lord led her down the unfamiliar road of persecution, accusation, ridicule, and shame. Jesus, Himself, consented to the unfamiliar when *He fell on his face, and prayed, saying, O my Father, if it be possible, let this cup pass from me: nevertheless not as I will, but as thou wilt (Matthew 26:39).* Both were at the crossroads of their lives; both had to make decisions that would determine and change their destinies and alter the course of history forever.

A decision must be made either to trust God and follow His lead or to remain in the same familiar, comfortable position. Oh, that our decisions would be made by faith and not by sight, which is most often deceiving!

*Jesus saith unto them...blessed are they that have not seen, and yet have believed (John 20:29).*

**Reflect on the following and then use the space provided to journal your thoughts.**
- *Locate yourself in the reading. What thoughts and feelings immediately come to mind?*
- *Did the passage of scripture help or challenge you in any way?*
- *Were you able to recognize the extension of God's love in this reading?*
- *What do you take away from the reading? How will you apply what you've read?*
- *What will you share with others?*

# A Place for Your Thoughts (Now ...)
## Crossroads

Date: _____

# A Place for Your Thoughts (Sometime later ...)
## Crossroads

Date:

# BEHIND THE SCENES

*For I know the plans I have for you, says the Lord. They are plans for good and not for disaster, to give you a future and a hope (Jeremiah 29:11 NLT).*

Unknown to us and without our permission, things are happening and plans are being made for our lives behind the scenes. God's plans for us generate movement in the spirit realm where our destiny begins and ends. Each movement is in sync with the will and timing of God for our yesterday, today, and tomorrow. Not visible to the natural eye, these sequential movements cannot be heard with the natural ear, nor can they be understood by the natural mind. *But as it is written, eye hath not seen, nor ear heard, neither have entered into the heart of man, the things which God hath prepared for them that love him (1 Corinthians 2:9).*

Therefore, since things are clearly out of our control and we have no ability of our own to manage things in the spirit realm, we must come to understand that the timing, the magnitude, and even the cessation of these movements are strictly overseen by God. Thus, we can breathe and let ourselves off the hook for not knowing it all and for not having it all together. God has it all under control; all we need to do is cooperate by submitting to His every instruction. He is fully capable of taking care of everything that concerns us. He is a vigilant watchman, always present making course corrections along our way so that we make it to our desired end. He remains awake in the night season. He never sleeps nor slumbers.

*He will not suffer thy foot to be moved: he that keepeth thee will not slumber (Psalm 121:3).*

**Reflect on the following and then use the space provided to journal your thoughts.**

- *Locate yourself in the reading. What thoughts and feelings immediately come to mind?*
- *Did the passage of scripture help or challenge you in any way?*
- *Were you able to recognize the extension of God's love in this reading?*
- *What do you take away from the reading? How will you apply what you've read?*
- *What will you share with others?*

# A Place for Your Thoughts (Now ...)
## Behind the Scenes

Date: _____

# A Place for Your Thoughts (Sometime later ...)
## Behind the Scenes

Date:

# WARNING - PAY CLOSE ATTENTION

*Therefore, we ought to give the more earnest heed to the things which we have heard, lest at any time we should let them slip (Hebrews 2:1).*

How easily our minds can wander. We can all recall times we have spent looking up at the stars, sitting on the patio enjoying a cool breeze, or just vegging out on the couch. These are called "no brainer" activities when our minds are in a state of "whatever." This state of mind is great when we are on vacation or having on-purpose down-time.

However, when it comes to the things of God, there is no down-time. Our spiritual senses must be constantly engaged, eyes attentive, ears ever listening, and our hearts open and receptive to what is being relayed to us by the Holy Spirit and through the Word of God. Christians should make it our goal to become surrounded by and enmeshed in the Word of God. This meshing keeps us aware and focused so our minds do not become randomly idle, and we do not drift away from the truth of God's Word. Paul said, *Be sober, be vigilant; because your adversary the devil, as a roaring lion, walketh about, seeking whom he may devour (1 Peter 5:8).* It has been penned that an idle mind is the devil's playground.

Paul, in his letter to Timothy gives this warning, *Now the Spirit expressly says that in latter times some will depart from the faith, giving heed to deceiving spirits and doctrines of demons (1 Timothy 4:1 NKJV).* This applies to every believer. *For false Christs and false prophets shall rise, and shall shew signs and wonders, to seduce, if it were possible, even the elect (Mark 13:22).* In these latter days, many are being deceived and seduced away from faith in Christ. We are surrounded by wolves in sheep's clothing speaking persuasive words, cultish religions, witchcraft, lust, greed, pride, and the pleasures of this world. Seduction comes when we take our eyes off Christ.

*Therefore, brethren, stand fast, and hold the traditions which ye have been taught, whether by word, or our epistle (2 Thessalonians 2:15).* These words ought to be the standard for all believers. Wavering is not an option. Compromise is not an option. Strength, stability, and steadfast determination are our only lines of defense. *For the time will come when they will not endure sound doctrine; but after their own lusts shall they heap to themselves teachers, having itching ears;_ And they shall turn away their ears from the truth, and shall be turned unto fables (2 Timothy 4:3-4).*

It is imperative that we are careful and watchful in what we see and hear. Our charge is to be selective in our associations, guarding who we allow in our lives and homes. The Holy Spirit will give us discernment, even with those who would offer to teach and pray for us. Our focus must be on the Lord. The things that we have read and the things we have learned regarding Christ and His Word must become our stability. *Holding fast the faithful word as he hath been taught, that he may be able by sound doctrine both to exhort and to convince the gainsayers (Titus 1:9).* **We are living in serious times. Serious times necessitate serious warnings.**

**Reflect on the following and then use the space provided to journal your thoughts.**

- *Locate yourself in the reading. What thoughts and feelings immediately come to mind?*
- *Did the passage of scripture help or challenge you in any way?*
- *Were you able to recognize the extension of God's love in this reading?*
- *What do you take away from the reading? How will you apply what you've read?*
- *What will you share with others?*

# A Place for Your Thoughts (Now ...)
## Warning

Date:

# A Place for Your Thoughts (Sometime later ...)
## Warning

Date:

# GOD'S LOVE COMFORTS THE SORROWFUL

*Then saith he unto them, my soul is exceeding sorrowful, even unto death:*
*tarry ye here and watch with me (Matthew 26:38).*

God's unspeakable love extends from Heaven to earth, resting upon the broken, battered, and bruised. At times of unspeakable pain and sorrow, only His love can touch the depth of our souls and bring comfort. During the time of His passion, Jesus was despised and rejected, filled with sorrow, and acquainted with tremendous grief. We can hear the depth of His sorrow when He prayed in the garden; *My soul is exceeding sorrowful, even unto death.* He sought comfort and compassion from His companions Peter, James, and John, but having no idea of the magnitude of His plight, they were not able to stay awake and pray through the night. Jesus sought for compassion when He asked, *O my Father, if it be possible, let his cup pass from me (Matthew 26:39).* His only comfort was the comfort of knowing that His Father loved Him and that He was fulfilling the purpose for which He was birthed into the earth.

We have not come to this place of sorrow and never will. However, there will be times in life that our sorrow and pain is so grievous we feel as though we are literally passing through the valley of the shadow of death (Psalm 23:4). It is especially in these times that the Father's great love for us and the compassionate heart of Jesus display themselves in our lives. Jesus, because of His passion, is able to meet our needs and to understand our grief. So, we must run to Him in times of great sorrow and unspeakable anguish. His arms of compassion are open wide, ready to receive any who would choose to come. *And Jesus went forth, and saw a great multitude, and was moved with compassion toward them, and he healed their sick (Matthew 14:14).*

It was never intended for us to experience or carry such pain and sorrow. Therefore, Jesus tells us to cast all our cares upon Him because He cares for us. He extends an invitation saying, *Come unto me, all ye that labour and are heavy laden, and I will give you rest (Matthew 11:28).*

Will you come?

**Reflect on the following and then use the space provided to journal your thoughts.**

- *Locate yourself in the reading. What thoughts and feelings immediately come to mind?*
- *Did the passage of scripture help or challenge you in any way?*
- *Were you able to recognize the extension of God's love in this reading?*
- *What do you take away from the reading? How will you apply what you've read?*
- *What will you share with others?*

# A Place for Your Thoughts (Now ...)
## The Sorrowful

Date: _____

# A Place for Your Thoughts (Sometime later ...)
## The Sorrowful

Date:

# GOD'S LOVE COVERS OUR SIN

*And above all things have fervent love for one another, for "love will cover a multitude of sins" (1 Peter 4:8 NKJV).*

God's love covers our sins; therefore, we should not be ashamed to come to Him in confession. Romans 3:23 states, *All have sinned and come short of the glory of God.* Interestingly enough, there are people who would disagree with this truth. They are the ones that say they have no sin; neither do they take responsibility for any wrongdoing in their lives. The Bible says, *If we say that we have no sin, we deceive ourselves, and the truth is not in us (1 John 1:8).*

Whatever the case, big sin, little sin, deliberate sin, white lies, occasional sin, half-truths, or exaggerations, they can all be forgiven. The acknowledgment of sin plays a vital role in our relationship with the Lord, *If we say that we have not sinned, we make him a liar, and his word is not in us (1 John 1:10).*

*I will go and return to my place, till they acknowledge their offence, and seek my face: in their affliction they will seek me early (Hosea 5:15).* God gave this response to Ephraim and Israel when they refused to acknowledge their sin. So, we see that time is important when it comes to repentance and acknowledging sin. The longer we wait to repent, the longer we remain under bondage to sin. *Know ye not, that to whom ye yield yourselves servants to obey, his servants ye are to whom ye obey; whether of sin unto death, or of obedience unto righteousness? (Romans 6:16)*

The choice is ours and the process is simple, *If we confess our sins, he is faithful and just to forgive us our sins, and to cleanse us from all unrighteousness (1 John 1:9).*

**Reflect on the following and then use the space provided to journal your thoughts.**

- *Locate yourself in the reading. What thoughts and feelings immediately come to mind?*
- *Did the passage of scripture help or challenge you in any way?*
- *Were you able to recognize the extension of God's love in this reading?*
- *What do you take away from the reading? How will you apply what you've read?*
- *What will you share with others?*

# A Place for Your Thoughts (Now ...)
## Our Sin

Date:

# A Place for Your Thoughts (Sometime later ...)
## Our Sin

Date:

# GOD'S LOVE DELIVERS

*He sent his word, and healed them, and delivered them from their destructions (Psalm 107:20).*

The Word of God delivers and rescues. The delivering power of the Word is activated in our lives by faith and by the words of our mouths. Revelation 12:11 says, *And they overcame him by the blood of the Lamb, and by the word of their testimony.* As we speak God's Word, His power goes out to back up our words and to bring us deliverance. Psalm 91:3-6 gives us this assurance, *Surely he shall deliver thee from the snare of the fowler, and from the noisome pestilence. He shall cover thee with his feathers, and under his wings shalt thou trust: his truth shall be thy shield and buckler. Thou shalt not be afraid for the terror by night; nor for the arrow that flieth by day; nor for the pestilence that walketh in darkness; nor for the destruction that wasteth at noonday.*

He also rescues us from our self-made destruction and unhealthy patterns of living. In our quest for maturity and independence, we can get into situations that are too deep for us to pull ourselves out of. It is often easier to be delivered from the apparent attacks of the enemy than it is to be delivered from our own personal strongholds and destructive ways. In our quest for a solution, we will only find two sets of answers: the wisdom of the world, *This wisdom descendeth not from above, but is earthly, sensual, devilish (James 3:15)* or wisdom from above, *But the wisdom that is from above is first pure, then peaceable, gentle, and easy to be intreated, full of mercy and good fruits, without partiality, and without hypocrisy (James 3:17).* Our choice determines our bondage or freedom.

Jesus taught His disciples to pray, *And lead us not into temptation, but deliver us from evil (Matthew 6:13).* Unfortunately, many do not recognize that they are bound and are in the midst of darkness. Therefore, they do not pray for deliverance nor seek to be rescued. In such cases, we can help our brothers by taking them before the Lord in prayer and intercession. *I exhort therefore, that, first of all, supplications, prayers, intercessions, and giving of thanks, be made for all men (1 Timothy 2:1).*

For the Christian, the keys to deliverance are acknowledgment and recognition. A heartfelt cry for help immediately brings the Rescuer into our situation. *He delivereth and rescueth, and he worketh signs and wonders in heaven and in earth (Daniel 6:27).*

**Reflect on the following and then use the space provided to journal your thoughts.**

- *Locate yourself in the reading. What thoughts and feelings immediately come to mind?*
- *Did the passage of scripture help or challenge you in any way?*
- *Were you able to recognize the extension of God's love in this reading?*
- *What do you take away from the reading? How will you apply what you've read?*
- *What will you share with others?*

# A Place for Your Thoughts (Now ...)
## Deliverance

Date: _____

# A Place for Your Thoughts (Sometime later ...)
## Deliverance

Date:

# GOD'S LOVE DISCERNS

*For the word of God is quick, and powerful, and sharper than any two-edged sword, piercing even to the dividing asunder of soul and spirit, and of the joints and marrow, and is a discerner of the thoughts and intents of the heart (Hebrews 4:12).*

The Word of God is a discerner of the thoughts and intents of our hearts. Discernment is critical to our success because God uses it to reveal to us the condition of our heart. He is omniscient and omnipresent, knowing and seeing everything, and is always everywhere. He sees beyond the camouflage, the facades, and the disguises we use to hide. *And there is no creature hidden from His sight, but all things are naked and open to the eyes of Him to whom we must give account (Hebrews 4:13 NKJV).*

Upon every examination and search of our hearts, there are adjustments and course corrections that must be made. *The spirit of man is the candle of the Lord, searching all the inward parts of the belly (Proverbs 20:27).* Adjustments are necessary to safeguard us against the pitfalls of the devil and to keep us on the right track with the will and plan of God. Those who choose to do regular self-examinations, keeping their thoughts, actions, and motives pure, will gain much reward as the Holy Spirit searches the reins of our hearts. *Examine yourselves, whether ye be in the faith; prove your own selves. Know ye not your own selves, how that Jesus Christ is in you, except ye be reprobates (2 Corinthians 13:5)?*

**Reflect on the following and then use the space provided to journal your thoughts.**

- *Locate yourself in the reading. What thoughts and feelings immediately come to mind?*
- *Did the passage of scripture help or challenge you in any way?*
- *Were you able to recognize the extension of God's love in this reading?*
- *What do you take away from the reading? How will you apply what you've read?*
- *What will you share with others?*

# A Place for Your Thoughts (Now ...)
## Discernment

Date:

# A Place for Your Thoughts (Sometime later ...)
## Discernment

Date: _____

# GOD'S LOVE IS EVERLASTING

*The Lord hath appeared of old unto me, saying, Yea, I have loved thee with an everlasting love; therefore with loving kindness have I drawn thee (Jeremiah 31:3).*

God's everlasting love towards us is enduring, uninterrupted, and perpetual. His love manifests itself in our lives through the extension of grace and mercy, through the blessings of peace and prosperity, and through our spiritual and physical strength on a daily basis. *Blessed be the Lord, who daily loadeth us with benefits (Psalm 68:19).*

His love is not to be compared with human love, which is both unstable and conditional. The question is asked in Romans 8:35. *Who shall separate us from the love of Christ? Shall tribulation, or distress, or persecution, or famine, or nakedness, or peril, or sword.* The answer follows in verses 38 and 39, *For I am persuaded, that neither death, nor life, nor angels, nor principalities, nor powers, nor things present, nor things to come, Nor height, nor depth, nor any other creature, shall be able to separate us from the love of God, which is in Christ Jesus our Lord.* Once received, there is no separation from His love. *For he hath said, I will never leave thee nor forsake thee (Hebrews 13:5).* Our natural minds have difficulty grasping a love that is so powerful and captivating.

The overwhelming nature of His love draws us to Him, and in turn, others are drawn to us as fruits of His love – goodness, kindness, joy, peace, patience, long-suffering, and temperance, are displayed in our lives. We have all experienced people being drawn to us for no apparent reason. Instantly, they want to be our best friend and hang around us all the time. They are drawn to the Christ in us. His love has the potential to draw both friends and enemies. Therefore, God uses His children to share and display His love with others who would dare to believe yet are not acquainted with Him. *But as many as received him, to them gave he the power to become the sons of God, even to them that believe on his name (John 1:12).*

**Reflect on the following and then use the space provided to journal your thoughts.**

- *Locate yourself in the reading. What thoughts and feelings immediately come to mind?*
- *Did the passage of scripture help or challenge you in any way?*
- *Were you able to recognize the extension of God's love in this reading?*
- *What do you take away from the reading? How will you apply what you've read?*
- *What will you share with others?*

# A Place for Your Thoughts (Now …)
## Everlasting

Date:

# A Place for Your Thoughts (Sometime later ...)
## Everlasting

Date:

# GOD'S LOVE GATHERS

*Not forsaking the assembling of ourselves together, as the manner of some is; but exhorting one another and so much the more, as ye see the day approaching (Hebrews 10:25).*

The day has arrived when the body of Christ "must" stand together exhorting and encouraging one another. *And let us consider one another to provoke unto love and to good works: Not forsaking the assembling of ourselves together, as the manner of some is; but exhorting one another: and so much the more, as ye see the day approaching (Hebrews 10:24-25).* Scripture instructs there be a gathering, an assemblage, a coming together of believers whose focus is Christ. It is essential for the welfare of the church. In these assemblies, the presence of God is manifested, and the power of God is at its highest. It is in these assemblies the saints are built up, encouraged, and their needs of support, guidance, healing, deliverance, exhortation, fellowship, and strength are met.

Each time there is a gathering, the Lord is present, *For where two or three are gathered together in my name, there am I in the midst of them (Matthew 18:20),* and *where the Spirit of the Lord is, there is liberty (2 Corinthians 3:17).* Not only is the Lord present, but His presence generates liberty: liberty to worship and praise, liberty to agree in prayer, liberty to be released from bondage, and liberty to open the sight of the blind. Miracles are dispensed! *And by the hands of the apostles were many signs and wonders wrought among the people; and they were all with one accord in Solomon's porch (Acts 5:12).*

The power of God fell upon the people as they gathered in the upper room. *And when the day of Pentecost was fully come, they were all with one accord in one place. And suddenly there came a sound from heaven as of a rushing mighty wind, and it filled all the house where they were sitting. And there appeared unto them cloven tongues like as of fire, and it sat upon each of them. And they were all filled with the Holy Ghost (Acts 2:1-4).*

While gathered at Mary's house praying for Peter, an Angel of the Lord released him from prison. *And, behold, the angel of the Lord came upon him, and a light shined in the prison: and he smote Peter on the side, and raised him up, saying, Arise up quickly. And his chains fell off from his hands. And the angel said unto him, Gird thyself, and bind on thy sandals. And he saith unto him, Cast thy garment about thee, and follow me...And when he had considered the thing, he came to the house of Mary the mother of John, whose surname was Mark; where many were gathered together praying (Acts 12: 7-8, 12).*

Let us be found in the gathering of the saints for this is where strength is renewed, and blessings are poured out. *Behold, how good and how pleasant it is for brethren to dwell together in unity! It is like the precious ointment upon the head, that ran down upon the beard, even Aaron's beard: that went down to the skirts of his garments; As the dew of Hermon, and as the dew that descended upon the mountains of Zion: for there the L*ord *commanded the blessing, even life for evermore (Psalm 133:1-3).*

**Reflect on the following and then use the space provided to journal your thoughts.**

- *Locate yourself in the reading. What thoughts and feelings immediately come to mind?*
- *Did the passage of scripture help or challenge you in any way?*
- *Were you able to recognize the extension of God's love in this reading?*
- *What do you take away from the reading? How will you apply what you've read?*
- *What will you share with others?*

# A Place for Your Thoughts (Now ...)
## Gathers

Date:

# A Place for Your Thoughts (Sometime later ...)
## Gathers

Date:

# GOD'S LOVE IS GENTLE

*Thou hast also given me the shield of thy salvation: and thy gentleness hath made me great (2 Samuel 22:36).*

God's gentle love is kind and tender, displaying a softness of action and effect. Contrary to man's opinion, He is not mean, harsh, or demanding, but rather a tenderhearted and loving Father, temperate in all things. When necessary, His hand brings correction without condemnation and mercy without judgment. The gentle correcting hand of a loving Father accomplishes more for His kingdom than the cruel hand of a hard taskmaster.

We are encouraged to step out in faith as the Holy Spirit directs us in the tasks and assignments which we have been given. We can accomplish them without the fear of failure, knowing that should we make a mistake, His gentleness will uphold us and make us great, *Thy right hand hath holden me up, and thy gentleness hath made me great (Psalm 18:35).*

**Reflect on the following and then use the space provided to journal your thoughts.**

- *Locate yourself in the reading. What thoughts and feelings immediately come to mind?*
- *Did the passage of scripture help or challenge you in any way?*
- *Were you able to recognize the extension of God's love in this reading?*
- *What do you take away from the reading? How will you apply what you've read?*
- *What will you share with others?*

# A Place for Your Thoughts (Now ...)
## The Gentleness of God

Date:

# A Place for Your Thoughts (Sometime later ...)
## The Gentleness of God

Date:

# GOD'S LOVE GIVES

*For God so loved the world, that He gave his only begotten Son, that whosoever believeth in Him should not perish, but have everlasting life (John 3:16).*

God's great love for mankind compelled Him to give the life of His only Son for us all. Jesus is the living demonstration of His love. It is without condition, restriction, or partiality. We find the written testimony of His love throughout the pages of the Bible, and we hear present-day testimonies of those whose lives have been changed by His grace.

God's ultimate gift of eternal life is free and available to all who choose to receive it by faith. However, there is only one way to get it, as stated in scripture. *That if thou shalt confess with thy mouth the Lord Jesus, and shalt believe in thine heart that God hath raised him from the dead, thou shalt be saved. For with the heart man believeth unto righteousness; and with the mouth confession is made unto salvation (Romans 10:9-10).* This is because there was only one sacrifice and only one man's blood was shed that we might live. That one person of whom the scripture speaks is Jesus Christ. Belief in Him is the only road that leads to eternal life. *Neither is there salvation in any other: for there is none other name under heaven given among men, whereby we must be saved (Acts 4:12).*

His love gave!

**Reflect on the following and then use the space provided to journal your thoughts.**

- *Locate yourself in the reading. What thoughts and feelings immediately come to mind?*
- *Did the passage of scripture help or challenge you in any way?*
- *Were you able to recognize the extension of God's love in this reading?*
- *What do you take away from the reading? How will you apply what you've read?*
- *What will you share with others?*

# A Place for Your Thoughts (Now ...)
## The Generosity of God

Date: _____

# A Place for Your Thoughts (Sometime later ...)
## The Generosity of God

Date:

# GOD'S LOVE UNDERSTANDS

*For we have not an high priest which cannot be touched with the feeling of our infirmities; but was in all points tempted like as we are, yet without sin (Hebrews 4:15).*

God understands when we are feeling some kind of way, and we cannot articulate it in words. The inability to express or even to identify what is really going on in our hearts is all too common. God knowing that at times we would be at a loss for words, gave us a helper in the person the Holy Spirit who regularly searches our hearts, *And he that searcheth the hearts knoweth what is the mind of the Spirit because he maketh intercession for the saints according to the will of God (Romans 8:27).* Through this search, the Spirit reveals to us what is in our hearts. He prays for us in His unique way; then, He gives us words to pray that put us in line with the Father's will for our lives.

The Word of God is a discerner of the thoughts and intentions of the heart; there is nothing that He does not already know. He knows and sees all things; nothing surprises Him. He will not judge us for our thoughts, good or bad. He will not condemn us for the anger, bitterness, or the disgust that we sometimes experience but rather gives this admonition, *"Be ye angry, and sin not: let not the sun go down upon your wrath" (Ephesians 4:26).* God is aware of our every emotion and *will bring to light the hidden things of darkness, and will make manifest the counsels of the heart (1 Corinthians 4:5),* so that healing and restoration can begin.

In those quiet moments when our eyes fill with tears, and our hearts cry out in frustration, He will cradle us in His loving arms of compassion. Such tender moments are too private to share as He catches every tear and lifts our hung down heads. *But thou, O LORD, art a shield for me; my glory, and the lifter up of mine head (Psalm 3:3).*

He understands like no other.

**Reflect on the following and then use the space provided to journal your thoughts.**

- *Locate yourself in the reading. What thoughts and feelings immediately come to mind?*
- *Did the passage of scripture help or challenge you in any way?*
- *Were you able to recognize the extension of God's love in this reading?*
- *What do you take away from the reading? How will you apply what you've read?*
- *What will you share with others?*

# A Place for Your Thoughts (Now …)
## Understanding

Date: _____

# A Place for Your Thoughts (Sometime later …)
## Understanding

Date:

# GOD'S LOVE HEALS

*But he was wounded for our transgressions, he was bruised for our iniquities: the chastisement of our peace was upon him; and with his stripes we are healed (Isaiah 53:5).*

The love of the Lord is so awesome and comprehensive that, at times, we cannot express it in words. This is the case when we consider the healing of our bodies. We cannot begin to imagine the extreme pain and agony experienced by Christ at Calvary for our redemption. The same pain and agony that brought us peace has also healed our bodies; w*ith His stripes we are healed (Isaiah 53:5).* It is beyond our understanding to imagine a love so great that one would openly and freely endure such suffering on behalf of another. Because of Christ's sacrifice, we are the recipients of a love that we may never understand.

There is no knowledge, skill, or intellect of man that can bring healing and cure without the intervention of Christ's sacrifice at Calvary. This healing encompasses our entire being, spirit, soul, and body, *Beloved, I wish above all things that thou mayest prosper and be in health, even as thy soul prospereth (3 John 2).* There is no explanation for this miracle except the extreme love of God for His created people. Therefore, it is required of us to turn our doubt into belief, to turn our murmuring into joy, and to accept the finished work of Christ at Calvary. This acceptance is what makes us whole. Extend your faith today. *Thy faith hath made thee whole; go in peace (Luke 8:48).*

**Reflect on the following and then use the space provided to journal your thoughts.**

- *Locate yourself in the reading. What thoughts and feelings immediately come to mind?*
- *Did the passage of scripture help or challenge you in any way?*
- *Were you able to recognize the extension of God's love in this reading?*
- *What do you take away from the reading? How will you apply what you've read?*
- *What will you share with others?*

# A Place for Your Thoughts (Now ...)
## Healing

Date: _____

# A Place for Your Thoughts (Sometime later ...)
## Healing

Date:

# GOD'S LOVE HEARS OUR CRIES

*The eyes of the Lord are upon the righteous, and his ears are open unto their cry (Psalm 34:15).*

You may be among those who feel as though God hears the prayers of some of His children more than He hears the prayers of others. If so, your thinking may need a little adjusting because our God is not a respecter of person. *For there is no respect of persons with God (Romans 2:11).* He hears us when we call, *I cried unto the LORD with my voice, and he heard me out of his holy hill (Psalm 3:4).*

Why then does it appear that certain prayers are answered and others not? Perhaps the answer lies in our personal hearing and our level of obedience. As God's children, we need not be jealous or concerned about others. God knows us by name, and He is well able to meet the individual needs of His children. That being so, perhaps we are addressing the wrong issue. Maybe our question ought to be, "Am I doing what is required of me in order to be blessed?" Are we operating according to James 1:22, *But be ye doers of the word, and not hearers only, deceiving your own selves?*

*In my distress I called upon the LORD and cried unto my God: he heard my voice out of his temple, and my cry came before him, even into his ears (Psalm 18:6).* God desires to hear the voice of His children so much that He has given us a shepherd who is diligent to make sure that our requests are heard. *For the eyes of the Lord are over the righteous, and his ears are open unto their prayers (1 Peter 3:12).*

When we take confidence in knowing that He has heard us, we can trust that our prayers will be answered. All we need do is wait. Cast not away therefore your confidence, which hath great recompense of reward. *For ye have need of patience, that, after ye have done the will of God, ye might receive the promise (Hebrews 10:35-36).*

**Reflect on the following and then use the space provided to journal your thoughts.**

- *Locate yourself in the reading. What thoughts and feelings immediately come to mind?*
- *Did the passage of scripture help or challenge you in any way?*
- *Were you able to recognize the extension of God's love in this reading?*
- *What do you take away from the reading? How will you apply what you've read?*
- *What will you share with others?*

# A Place for Your Thoughts (Now ...)
## Our Cries

Date: _____

# A Place for Your Thoughts (Sometime later ...)
## Our Cries

Date:

# HE'S IN THERE!

*And I will pray the Father, and he shall give you another Comforter, that he may abide with you forever (John 14:16).*

My car pulls into the driveway, the engine warm from the trip home. It's been a long day on the job with much conversation and decisions to make. The drive home was uneventful, with the exception of the usual traffic and road rage. As I gather my personal items and belongings, the thought runs through my mind, "He's in there!"

He's waiting right on the other side of the door. The anticipation builds as I close the car door, mount the steps, and place my key into the lock. Instantly, I smell His fragrance; the atmosphere welcomes me home as the Father's love and peace engulf my heart. I am in His presence.

There is no solace greater than finding the presence of God awaiting you in your own home. Peace may be found in other places; however, to have it be a resident in your home is sheer delight. Jesus said, *"Behold, I stand at the door, and knock: if any man hear my voice, and open the door, I will come in to him, and will sup with him, and he with me (Rev. 3:20)."* His desire is to come and abide with us forever. *Lo, I am with you alway, even unto the end of the world. Amen (Mathew 28:20).*

In quiet times, He will knock. In the midst of prayer and heartfelt praise, He will knock. In times of trouble and sorrow or chaos and confusion, He will knock. Be sure to answer the door; He will not come in uninvited. Once in, He will abide with you forever. His purpose is not to be a causal visitor nor a part-time tenant, but rather a permanent resident. Listen for the knock; it will surely come.

**Reflect on the following and then use the space provided to journal your thoughts.**

- *Locate yourself in the reading. What thoughts and feelings immediately come to mind?*
- *Did the passage of scripture help or challenge you in any way?*
- *Were you able to recognize the extension of God's love in this reading?*
- *What do you take away from the reading? How will you apply what you've read?*
- *What will you share with others?*

# A Place for Your Thoughts (Now ...)
## The Presence of God

Date:

# A Place for Your Thoughts (Sometime later ...)
## The Presence of God

Date:

# I AM A WINNER!

*Now thanks be unto God, which always causeth us to triumph in Christ*
*(2 Corinthians 2:14).*

In a recently read article, this question was asked, "Are you a Winner?" My immediate response was, "Yes, I am a winner!" I did not have to think about it or hesitate because I knew the answer. I did not have to become a winner; I was already one. Winners do not win every battle, conquer every foe, or always come out on top. Winners submit to the Lord, who fights for them. Winners rest in peace by placing their hope and trust in the Lord, and finally, winners allow the light of Christ to shine forth in them so that others will see their good works and glorify God (Matthew 5:16).

What makes one a winner? To qualify as a winner, several components have to be in operation. The first is the acceptance of Jesus Christ as Lord and Savior. This acceptance automatically draws us into a covenant position, which grants us full access to the heart of the Father. Having His heart means also having His ear when you call, when you pray, and when you seek. Who could ask for anything more? *And if we know that he hears us, whatsoever we ask, we know that we have the petitions that we desired of him (1 John 5:15).*

Second is the stabilizing structure of scripture. The written Word of God must have preeminence, and the final say in every situation. In times of sadness, grief, and deep trouble, the Word of God anchors the mind and emotions with the tremendous force of truth. The Word of God can address every situation that we will ever encounter. When used correctly, it is a powerful, sharp weapon in the life of the believer. *For the word of God is quick, and powerful, and sharper than any two-edged sword, piercing even to the dividing asunder of soul and spirit, and of the joints and marrow, and is a discerner of the thoughts and intents of the heart (Hebrews 4:12).*

The final component that assures our victory and causes us to be a winner is faithfulness. God delights in displays of faithfulness, loving your neighbor, praying for your enemies, giving cheerfully, ministering to the poor, etc. Faithfulness is also a determining factor regarding our entrance into Heaven. *His lord said unto him, Well done, thou good and faithful servant; thou hast been faithful over a few things, I will make thee ruler over many things: enter thou into the joy of thy lord (Matthew 25:21).* Simply put, winners have Christ as Lord, winners live by the Word of God, and winners are faithful servants. Do you fit this description? If so, then you too are a winner!

**Reflect on the following and then use the space provided to journal your thoughts.**

- *Locate yourself in the reading. What thoughts and feelings immediately come to mind?*
- *Did the passage of scripture help or challenge you in any way?*
- *Were you able to recognize the extension of God's love in this reading?*
- *What do you take away from the reading? How will you apply what you've read?*
- *What will you share with others?*

# A Place for Your Thoughts (Now ...)
## A Winner!

Date:

# A Place for Your Thoughts (Sometime later ...)
## A Winner!

Date:

# IN HIS TIME

*To everything there is a season, and a time to every purpose under the heaven (Ecclesiastes 3:1).*

After months and months of waiting, my daughter's application process for a program important for her future was finally complete. The waiting process was long, during which time she fought off seasons of stress, anxiety, and discouragement. At times, she questioned if this was really God's plan or if this was really the direction for her life. Finally, the letter arrived with the words "fully favorable" written on the recommendation. That was it! She had been accepted without opposition. The wait was now over. The acceptance came in God's perfect timing bringing with it: peace of mind, open doors, and financial security.

There is a common saying among Christians, "I'm waiting on the Lord; He is always right on time." It sounds really good, but most find that waiting is not as easy as it sounds. Could it be that there is a difference between man's perception and God's perception of time? Man judges time in increments of 24 hours in a day. Seven days become a week; weeks turn into months, and months into years. Our impatience shows up when the days, weeks, months, and years pass without the manifestation of answered prayer. We all have the tendency to become discouraged. *Hope deferred makes the heart sick (Proverbs 13:12 NKJV).*

God's perception of time is described in 2 Peter 3:8 (NIV). *But do not forget this one thing, dear friends: With the Lord a day is like a thousand years, and a thousand years are like a day.* Are we to believe there are a thousand years between the beginning of each new day at 12:01 am to the close of the same day at 11:59 pm? Even the most intellectual and scientific minds cannot comprehend a thousand years in terms of one day. This concept is a mind-boggling example of Isaiah 55:8-9, *For my thoughts are not your thoughts, neither are your ways my ways, saith the LORD. For as the heavens are higher than the earth, so are my ways higher than your ways, and my thoughts than your thoughts.* We can see there is a clear difference between God's timing and our timing, which lends itself to the impatience of man, yet accounts for God being right on time.

Let us take a look at the life of Abraham and Sarah in Genesis 16. God told them they would, at some point, have a son. After many years of bareness, they decided to do things their way, and Abraham fathered a child by his wife's concubine. This was not the child promised them of the Lord. This child, Ishmael, was the son of impatience, and with his birth, strife, jealousy, and distress entered their home. In God's time, the child of promise, Isaac, was born naturally to Abraham and Sarah. God was true to His word. It is to our advantage to find satisfaction and solace in waiting. Waiting is easier than trying to make things happen on our own and paying the price for impatience. Wait for the appointed time. *And the LORD appointed a set time, saying, To morrow the LORD shall do this thing in the land (Exodus 9:5).*

The key to waiting and getting in sync with God's timing is patience. *But let patience have her perfect work, that ye may be perfect and entire, wanting nothing (James 1:4).*

**Reflect on the following and then use the space provided to journal your thoughts.**
- *Locate yourself in the reading. What thoughts and feelings immediately come to mind?*
- *Did the passage of scripture help or challenge you in any way?*
- *Were you able to recognize the extension of God's love in this reading?*
- *What do you take away from the reading? How will you apply what you've read?*
- *What will you share with others?*

# A Place for Your Thoughts (Now ...)
## An On-Time God

Date:

# A Place for Your Thoughts (Sometime later ...)
## An On-Time God

Date:

# GOD'S LOVE INFUSED

*Herein is love, not that we loved God, but that he loved us, and sent his Son to be the propitiation for our sins. Beloved, if God so loved us, we ought also to love one another (1 John 4:10-11).*

The love of God infuses our hearts so much that we cry out, "I love You, I love You, Lord." Every believer should possess a deep love for their God, a love that is birthed out of God's love for us. *We love him, because he first loved us (1 John 4:19).* No one can take credit for loving God first as there is no real love, only counterfeit love, without the initial extension of His love toward us. Without Him, we would not know love.

Knowing this takes away the conditions and the limitations man has placed on love. True God infused love is unconditional, having no limits or boundaries. Two simple questions need to be answered. Are you loved unconditionally by God, and are you loving others with that same unconditional love? *A new commandment I give unto you, That ye love one another; as I have loved you, that ye also love one another (John 13:34).*

Think about it.

**Reflect on the following and then use the space provided to journal your thoughts.**

- *Locate yourself in the reading. What thoughts and feelings immediately come to mind?*
- *Did the passage of scripture help or challenge you in any way?*
- *Were you able to recognize the extension of God's love in this reading?*
- *What do you take away from the reading? How will you apply what you've read?*
- *What will you share with others?*

# A Place for Your Thoughts (Now ...)
## Unconditional Love

Date:

# A Place for Your Thoughts (Sometime later ...)
## Unconditional Love

Date: _____

# GOD'S LOVE INTERCEDES

*It is Christ that died, yea rather, that is risen again, who is even at the right hand of God, who also maketh intercession for us (Romans 8:34).*

Christ is now seated at the right hand of the Father in the heavens, making intercession for the saints. His righteousness bridges the gap between the Father and us. *My little children, these things write I unto you, that ye sin not. And if any man sin, we have an advocate with the Father, Jesus Christ the righteous (1 John 2:1).* Even when we confess our sins and walk in the way of righteousness scripture says, *But we are all as an unclean thing, and all our righteousness are as filthy rags (Isaiah 64:6).* It is only through the righteous veil of Christ that we will ever be seen by the Father.

The love of Christ also stands in the gap between our sin and the enemy's desire to devour us. His express purpose is to steal, kill, and destroy (John 10:10). As human beings made from the dust of the earth, we are physically powerless against the evil forces of darkness that come to plague our lives. Without Christ's intercession, we would perish. It was His love that interceded for us in the garden upon the occasion of Adam's sin. His love interceded for us when the earth was filled with sin and covered over with the flood of Noah. His love interceded in Gethsemane through the time of His passion and ultimately at Calvary. His love interceded as the Holy Spirt was poured out on the Day of Pentecost, and His love still intercedes for us today.

It stands as a sentry guarding and watching over us every moment of the day and night. *When the enemy shall come in like a flood, the Spirit of the LORD shall lift up a standard against him (Isaiah 59:19).* When we *walk through the valley of the shadow of death (Psalm 23:4), we will fear no evil,* because He is with us, and the promise of Psalm 91:15 will cover us, *I will be with him in trouble; I will deliver him, and honour him.*

The spiritual and physical intercession of Christ has saved those who believe in Him from the reward of sin, eternal damnation. *Wherefore he is able also to save them to the uttermost that come unto God by him, seeing he ever liveth to make intercession for them (Hebrews 7:25).*

**Reflect on the following and then use the space provided to journal your thoughts.**

- *Locate yourself in the reading. What thoughts and feelings immediately come to mind?*
- *Did the passage of scripture help or challenge you in any way?*
- *Were you able to recognize the extension of God's love in this reading?*
- *What do you take away from the reading? How will you apply what you've read?*
- *What will you share with others?*

# A Place for Your Thoughts (Now ...)
## Intercession

Date:

# A Place for Your Thoughts (Sometime later ...)
## Intercession

Date:

# LIFE INTERRUPTED

*The steps of a good man are ordered by the Lord: and he delighteth in his way*
*(Psalm 37:23).*

Just when you have it all figured out, plans are coming together, and life is on track according to your schedule, enter interruption. Interruptions are those unexpected and often unpleasant situations and issues that arise out of nowhere. Depending upon the situation, interruptions, good or bad, can alter plans, and most times, cause things to go awry by creating temporary delays and setbacks. However, we must never lose sight of the original purpose. We must press forward until the goal is achieved.

What about the visions and plans that we know beyond a shadow of a doubt have come from the Lord? Surely, they are not subject to interruption. Scripture does state, *The steps of a good man are ordered by the Lord (Psalm 37:23).* However, it does not say the steps would be without interruption. Look at Mary, the mother of Jesus, whose plan was to quietly become the wife of Joseph. Imagine the wedding plans were all set, guests were invited, food was being prepared, the dress was ready, and out of the blue the angel of the Lord appeared saying, *Fear not, Mary: for thou hast found favour with God. And, behold, thou shalt conceive in thy womb, and bring forth a son, and shalt call his name JESUS (Luke 1:30-31).* Life Interrupted!

Paul the Apostle was going about his life seeking the kingdom and preaching the good news of Christ when he revealed, *There was given to me a thorn in the flesh, the messenger of Satan to buffet me, lest I should be exalted above measure. For this thing I besought the Lord thrice, that it might depart from me. And he said unto me, My grace is sufficient for thee: for my strength is made perfect in weakness (2 Corinthians 12:7-9).* Life interrupted! In spite of Paul's many interruptions, he continued to do the will of the Father, declaring at the end of his life, *I have fought a good fight, I have finished my course, I have kept the faith (2 Timothy 4:7).*

Then, we see Jesus, who at the onset of His public ministry, being baptized in water and in the Holy Ghost was immediately, *led of the Spirit into the wilderness to be tempted of the devil (Matthew 4:1).* Life interrupted! Three years later, Jesus uttered these words, *it is finished (John 19:30).*

God, who is omniscient (knowing all things) and omnipresent (everywhere at the same time), is not at all shocked or surprised by the things that we encounter along life's journey. Interruptions from people, the devil, everyday trials of life, and from God come to prove and to test our faith. We must not become angry, discouraged, or faint but rather be sober, vigilant, flexible, and teachable. Courage and patience are required so that we too may finish our course and receive the rewards laid up for us. *Blessed is the man that endureth temptation: for when he is tried, he shall receive the crown of life, which the Lord hath promised to them that love him (James 1:12).*

*A Side Note*

Let us remain free of any guilt or self-condemnation when faced with interruptions. They are not the result of a lack of faith; neither are they a result of an abundance of faith as understood in Ecclesiastes 9:11, *I returned, and saw under the sun, that the race is not to the swift, nor the battle to the strong, neither yet bread to the wise, nor yet riches to men of understanding, nor yet favour to men of skill; but time and chance happeneth to them all.*

**Reflect on the following and then use the space provided to journal your thoughts.**

- *Locate yourself in the reading. What thoughts and feelings immediately come to mind?*
- *Did the passage of scripture help or challenge you in any way?*
- *Were you able to recognize the extension of God's love in this reading?*
- *What do you take away from the reading? How will you apply what you've read?*
- *What will you share with others?*

# A Place for Your Thoughts (Now ...)
## Life's Interruptions

Date: _____

# A Place for Your Thoughts (Sometime later …)
## Life's Interruptions

Date:

# GOD'S LOVE MANIFESTED

*For the life was manifested, and we have seen it, and bear witness, and shew unto you that eternal life, which was with the Father, and was manifested unto us (1 John 1:2).*

God's love is seen and experienced in our lives through the manifestation of His actions towards us. His actions are always good. Though we may not always understand why God does what He does, we can be assured that whatever He does is for our good. *For I know the plans I have for you, says the Lord. They are plans for good and not for disaster, to give you a future and a hope (Jeremiah 29:11 NLT).*

The display of His love is not just spiritual; there are natural manifestations that shape our lives in ways too numerous to count. His love is poured out and lavished on us so much that the question was asked, *What is man, that You art mindful of him, And the son of man that You visit him (Psalm 8:4 NKJV)?* His daily outpouring of love delivers us from evil, opens blinded eyes, heals diseased bodies, and comforts hearts in times of grief. He leads us beside still waters, restores our soul, lifts up hung down heads, and hides us in secret places. It forgives sins, supplies needs, mends relationships, rebukes the devourer, and answers every prayer. His love never fails. *In this was manifested the love of God toward us, because that God sent his only begotten Son into the world, that we might live through him (1 John 4:9).*

His love for us is perfect. His plans are excellent. Therefore, we are without excuse when it comes to loving our fellow man. The strength and covering of His mercy alone afford us the grace to love. *Let love be without dissimulation. Abhor that which is evil; cleave to that which is good. Be kindly affectioned one to another with brotherly love; in honour preferring one another (Romans 12:9-10).* We are an extension of His love poured out.

**Reflect on the following and then use the space provided to journal your thoughts.**

- *Locate yourself in the reading. What thoughts and feelings immediately come to mind?*
- *Did the passage of scripture help or challenge you in any way?*
- *Were you able to recognize the extension of God's love in this reading?*
- *What do you take away from the reading? How will you apply what you've read?*
- *What will you share with others?*

# A Place for Your Thoughts (Now ...)
## Love Manifested

Date:

# A Place for Your Thoughts (Sometime later ...)
## Love Manifested

Date:

# GOD'S LOVE IS PATIENT

*The servant therefore fell down, and worshipped him, saying, Lord, have patience with me (Matthew 18:26).*

God's love is always patient towards His children. His patience is accompanied by goodness, longsuffering, forbearance, and the extension of kindness. Should we consider how often we have said, "Lord, have patience with me," we might become weary and faint in our minds. Yet, upon each occasion, His answer is always a resounding, "Yes."

On the other side of the coin, how patient are we with God? Do we find ourselves murmuring and complaining while He is busy working things out on our behalf? Do we offer impatient excuses and throw temper tantrums, hoping to speed up the process? Let us consider the words in James 1:2-4, *My brethren, count it all joy when ye fall into divers temptations; Knowing this, that the trying of your faith worketh patience. But let patience have her perfect work, that ye may be perfect and entire, wanting nothing.* We must remind ourselves that things in life are not always a quick fix. But we can rest in the assurance that our patience will always yield a reward. *Cast not away therefore your confidence, which hath great recompence of reward. For ye have need of patience, that, after ye have done the will of God, ye might receive the promise. For yet a little while, and he that shall come will come, and will not tarry (Hebrews 10:35-37).*

**Reflect on the following and then use the space provided to journal your thoughts.**

- *Locate yourself in the reading. What thoughts and feelings immediately come to mind?*
- *Did the passage of scripture help or challenge you in any way?*
- *Were you able to recognize the extension of God's love in this reading?*
- *What do you take away from the reading? How will you apply what you've read?*
- *What will you share with others?*

# A Place for Your Thoughts (Now ...)
## Patience

Date:

# A Place for Your Thoughts (Sometime later ...)
## Patience

Date:

# GOD'S LOVE PRODUCES FRUIT

*But the fruit of the Spirit is love, joy, peace, longsuffering, gentleness, goodness, faith, meekness, temperance (Galatians 5:22-23).*

God's love towards us is alive and productive. God's love in us bears much fruit. *But the fruit of the Spirit is love, joy, peace, longsuffering, gentleness, goodness, faith, meekness, and temperance (Galatians 5: 22-23)*, are all manifestations of His character. They should be the goal of every Christian. We are predestined; our lives are set up to be conformed to His image. Part of the conformity is the development of the fruit of the Spirit. Those created in His image will produce the same kind of fruits. By this they will know that we are His children, *For every tree is known by his own fruit (Luke 6:44).*

Because spiritual fruit cannot begin to develop or be sustained on its own, we must be connected to Jesus. He said, *I am the vine, ye are the branches: He that abideth in me, and I in him, the same bringeth forth much fruit: for without me ye can do nothing (John 15:5).* Time spent in His presence and in submission to His Word causes us to become conformed to His image and to His character. This is how others will know that we are of Christ. *Wherefore by their fruits ye shall know them (Matthew 7:20).*

**Reflect on the following and then use the space provided to journal your thoughts.**

- *Locate yourself in the reading. What thoughts and feelings immediately come to mind?*
- *Did the passage of scripture help or challenge you in any way?*
- *Were you able to recognize the extension of God's love in this reading?*
- *What do you take away from the reading? How will you apply what you've read?*
- *What will you share with others?*

# A Place for Your Thoughts (Now ...)
## Spiritual Fruit

Date: _____

# A Place for Your Thoughts (Sometime later ...)
## Spiritual Fruit

Date:

# GOD'S LOVE PROVIDES

*But my God shall supply all your need according to His riches in glory by Christ Jesus (Philippians 4:19).*

Everyday provision is made for the children of God. Jesus taught His disciples to pray, *Give us this day our daily bread (Matthew 6:11).* Paul, in writing to the Philippians said, *Be careful for nothing; but in everything by prayer and supplication with thanksgiving let your requests be made known unto God. And the peace of God, which passeth all understanding, shall keep your hearts and minds through Christ Jesus (Philippians 4:6-7).* God delights in meeting the needs of His children and has more than enough riches and resources to back up His invitation. *For every beast of the forest is mine, and the cattle upon a thousand hills. I know all the fowls of the mountains: and the wild beasts of the field are mine (Psalm 50:10-11).*

Be careful for nothing means essentially what it says; there is no reason God's children should lack anything. All we need to do is ask; however, many hesitate and find it difficult to ask. Feelings of unworthiness, shame, guilt, independence, false humility, and the lies of the enemy have kept many in a place of lack and want. But we know that is not God's plan for His children. Be encouraged to come to Him boldly regardless of the situation, and you will find help and resources in abundance. *Now he that ministereth seed to the sower both minister bread for your food, and multiply your seed sown, and increase the fruits of your righteousness; being enriched in everything to all bountifulness, which causeth through us thanksgiving to God (2 Corinthians 9:10-11).*

**Reflect on the following and then use the space provided to journal your thoughts.**

- *Locate yourself in the reading. What thoughts and feelings immediately come to mind?*
- *Did the passage of scripture help or challenge you in any way?*
- *Were you able to recognize the extension of God's love in this reading?*
- *What do you take away from the reading? How will you apply what you've read?*
- *What will you share with others?*

# A Place for Your Thoughts (Now ...)
## Love Provides

Date:

# A Place for Your Thoughts (Sometime later ...)
## Love Provides

Date:

# GOD'S LOVE IS RECIPROCAL

*This is my commandment, that ye love one another, as I have loved you (John 15:12).*

Love is created to be reciprocal. God loves us, and we love Him in return. Our relationship with the Lord was made to be give and take. The same principle applies in a love relationship between a man and a woman. *Therefore, shall a man leave his father and his mother, and shall cleave unto his wife: and they shall be one flesh (Genesis 2:24).* In like manner, we are to leave our relationship with the world and cleave unto Christ, *but he that is joined unto the Lord is one spirit (1 Corinthians 6:17).*

Husbands and wives marry, sealing their commitment with a vow to love one another in good times and in bad, for better or for worse, and in sickness and in health until they are separated by death. This is a very strong bond. In a like manner, God pledges His love for us with a vow, *For he hath said, I will never leave thee, nor forsake thee (Hebrews 13:5).* Romans 8:28-39 gives a picture of our bond and love connection with the Lord, *For I am persuaded, that neither death, nor life, nor angels, nor principalities, nor powers, nor things present, nor things to come, Nor height, nor depth, nor any other creature, shall be able to separate us from the love of God, which is in Christ Jesus our Lord.* This is genuine love.

The Apostle Paul sealed his love for the Lord by remaining faithful throughout his missionary journeys. He proved his love *in afflictions, in necessities, in distresses, in stripes, in imprisonments, in tumults, in labours, in watchings, in fastings, by pureness, by knowledge, by longsuffering (2 Corinthians 2:4-6),* and by his acts of kindness and his love for the brethren. In turn, God proved His love for Paul by the manifestations of miracles, signs, and wonders. Paul was not hurt when he ate deadly things. He did not die when bitten by poisonous snakes. He survived being shipwrecked three times and a multitude of other challenges. But through it all, they (Paul and Christ) were faithful to one another. A powerful example of the power of reciprocal love. *We love him, because he first loved us (1 John 4:19).*

Will you love Him in return?

**Reflect on the following and then use the space provided to journal your thoughts.**

- *Locate yourself in the reading. What thoughts and feelings immediately come to mind?*
- *Did the passage of scripture help or challenge you in any way?*
- *Were you able to recognize the extension of God's love in this reading?*
- *What do you take away from the reading? How will you apply what you've read?*
- *What will you share with others?*

# A Place for Your Thoughts (Now ...)
## Reciprocity

Date:

# A Place for Your Thoughts (Sometime later ...)
## Reciprocity

Date:

# GOD'S LOVE SEEKS TRUE WORSHIPPERS

*The hour cometh, and now is, when true worshippers shall worship the Father in spirit and in truth (John 4:23).*

The Lord seeks true worshippers to worship Him in spirit and in truth. True worship is more than just words and expressions of praise but rather a commitment of the heart and mind in seeking the Lord in all your ways. *When thou saidst, Seek ye my face; my heart said unto thee, your face, Lord, will I seek (Psalm 27:8).*

This is the commitment the Lord is looking for with His children as He draws them unto Himself. As in any relationship, there are ups and downs, trials and errors, and joy and sorrow. However, those who are willing to make the commitment and become true worshippers will never be disappointed.

*Exalt ye the LORD our God, and worship at his footstool (Psalm 99:5).*

**Reflect on the following and then use the space provided to journal your thoughts.**

- *Locate yourself in the reading. What thoughts and feelings immediately come to mind?*
- *Did the passage of scripture help or challenge you in any way?*
- *Were you able to recognize the extension of God's love in this reading?*
- *What do you take away from the reading? How will you apply what you've read?*
- *What will you share with others?*

# A Place for Your Thoughts (Now ...)
## True Worshippers

Date:

# A Place for Your Thoughts (Sometime later ...)
## True Worshippers

Date:

# GOD'S LOVE RESTORES LIFE

*And he said unto me, Son of man, can these bones live? And I answered,*
*O Lord God, thou knowest (Ezekiel 37:3).*

Life's situations can bring such disappointment, dryness, discouragement, and even depression. All four of these have the ability to go into hiding and to continue for years undetected. However, there does come a point when their existence becomes apparent. Lack of energy, loss of identity and purpose, no desire for God, anger, and isolation, leading to depression, hopelessness, and despair. *A broken spirit drieth the bones (Prov 17:22).*

What is our response to be when we recognize this condition in ourselves or in others? When asked if the dry bones could live, the prophet Ezekiel gave a wise answer. *O Lord God, thou knowest (Ezekiel 37:3).* This answer was wise because only God knows the condition of a person's heart. On our own, we have no solution for a hurting heart. Our job is to be filled with compassion and to lead people to the feet of Jesus, who is the healer and the mender of broken hearts. *The Spirit of the Lord GOD is upon me; because the LORD hath anointed me to preach good tidings unto the meek; he hath sent me to bind up the brokenhearted, to proclaim liberty to the captives, and the opening of the prison to them that are bound (Isaiah 61:1).* Only He can turn around the grave of despair. Only He can restore life to a broken spirit and cause a person's heart to live again.

Oh, Lord, restore my soul!

**Reflect on the following and then use the space provided to journal your thoughts.**

- *Locate yourself in the reading. What thoughts and feelings immediately come to mind?*
- *Did the passage of scripture help or challenge you in any way?*
- *Were you able to recognize the extension of God's love in this reading?*
- *What do you take away from the reading? How will you apply what you've read?*
- *What will you share with others?*

# A Place for Your Thoughts (Now ...)
## Restoration

Date:

# A Place for Your Thoughts (Sometime later ...)
## Restoration

Date:

# GOD'S LOVE UNIFIES

*Endeavoring to keep the unity of the Spirit in the bond of peace (Ephesians 4:3).*

God's amazing love is focused on unifying the body of Christ worldwide. Ephesians 4:11-13 explains that God has set leaders in the church to help it grow in unity. *And he gave some, apostles; and some, prophets; and some, evangelists; and some, pastors and teachers; For the perfecting of the saints, for the work of the ministry, for the edifying of the body of Christ: Till we all come in the unity of the faith, and of the knowledge of the Son of God, unto a perfect man, unto the measure of the stature of the fulness of Christ:*

Simply stated, all believers must come to a place of unity and agreement concerning what we believe and teach. Man, unfortunately in his earthly wisdom, has divided the church according to denominations, ethnicities, skin color, tradition, and personal beliefs. A divided church is not God's plan. *Again, the kingdom of heaven is like unto a net, that was cast into the sea, and gathered of every kind (Matthew 13:47).* It is the Father's desire that his children come together as one in His name and under the banner of His love. This is expressed in the following passages of scripture:

*There is one body, and one Spirit, even as ye are called in one hope of your calling; One Lord, one faith, one baptism, One God and Father of all, who is above all, and through all, and in you all (Ephesians 4:4-6).*

*There is neither Jew nor Greek, there is neither bond nor free, there is neither male nor female: for ye are all one in Christ Jesus (Galatians 3:28).*

The social climate of the time we live in coupled with the unruly behavior we observe could tend to make one think and declare that "peace is not possible." However, our God specializes in making the impossible possible. Jesus said unto him, *If thou canst believe, all things are possible to him that believeth (Mark 9:23).* Our part is to only believe.

*Behold, how good and how pleasant it is for brethren to dwell together in unity! (Psalm 133:1)*

**Reflect on the following and then use the space provided to journal your thoughts.**

- *Locate yourself in the reading. What thoughts and feelings immediately come to mind?*
- *Did the passage of scripture help or challenge you in any way?*
- *Were you able to recognize the extension of God's love in this reading?*
- *What do you take away from the reading? How will you apply what you've read?*
- *What will you share with others?*

# A Place for Your Thoughts (Now ...)
## Unity

Date:

# A Place for Your Thoughts (Sometime later ...)
## Unity

Date:

# GOD'S LOVE SATISFIES THE THIRSTY

*O God, thou art my God; early will I seek thee: my soul thirsteth for thee, my flesh longeth for thee in a dry and thirsty land, where no water is (Psalm 63:1).*

Only the love of God can satisfy the thirsty soul. In John 4:10, Jesus addressed the woman at the well saying, *"If you knew the gift of God and who it is that asks you for a drink, you would have asked Him and he would have given you living water (John 4:10 NIV)."* Jesus lived and ministered on earth as the fountain of living water. He constantly poured Himself out to all that would dare to come unto Him and drink. *For every one that asketh receiveth; and he that seeketh findeth; and to him that knocketh it shall be opened (Matthew 7:8).*

When we ask something of the Lord, it is imperative that we are specific in our request, as was the woman in Matthew 9:20-22. *And, behold, a woman, which was diseased with an issue of blood twelve years, came behind him, and touched the hem of his garment: For she said within herself, If I may but touch his garment, I shall be whole. But Jesus turned him about, and when he saw her, he said, Daughter, be of good comfort; thy faith hath made thee whole. And the woman was made whole from that hour.* This woman was seeking the living water to quench her thirst, heal her body, and make her whole.

That same living water is available to all who thirst. *For I will pour water upon him that is thirsty, and floods upon the dry ground (Isaiah 44:3).* **Asking is the key to the release of living water in our lives.** The moment we open the door of our hearts to the Lord, water is poured out, and our thirst is quenched.

Ask for the living water.

**Reflect on the following and then use the space provided to journal your thoughts.**

- *Locate yourself in the reading. What thoughts and feelings immediately come to mind?*
- *Did the passage of scripture help or challenge you in any way?*
- *Were you able to recognize the extension of God's love in this reading?*
- *What do you take away from the reading? How will you apply what you've read?*
- *What will you share with others?*

# A Place for Your Thoughts (Now ...)
## Thirst

Date:

# A Place for Your Thoughts (Sometime later ...)
## Thirst

Date:

# GOD'S LOVE SEARCHES

*Now He who searches the hearts knows what the mind of the Spirit is, because He makes intercession for the saints according to the will of God (Romans 8:27 NKJV).*

God's love searches our hearts and our souls. He knows our minds better than we do. The Holy Spirit, who is the Spirit of Truth, knows all things, and through this knowledge, Jesus Christ makes intercession for us. *Wherefore he is able also to save them to the uttermost that come unto God by him, seeing he ever liveth to make intercession for them (Hebrews 7:25).*

This Spirit's search reveals that our own hearts can, at times, be most wicked. Through Christ's intercession, the stony heart can transform into a compassionate heart of flesh enabling us to show love and compassion for one another. *A new heart also will I give you, and a new spirit will I put within you: and I will take away the stony heart out of your flesh, and I will give you an heart of flesh (Ezekiel 36:26).*

The Spirit's searching, Christ's intercession, and our obedience are the catalyst that set Romans 8:26 in motion. *But the Spirit itself maketh intercession for us with groanings which cannot be uttered. And he that searcheth the hearts knoweth what is the mind of the Spirit, because he maketh intercession for the saints according to the will of God.* Again, the trio, searching, intercession, and obedience, are essential when it comes to fulfilling purpose and experiencing the fullness of God's blessing in our lives. Submit to the search!

*And we know that all things work together for good to them that love God, to them who are the called according to his purpose (Romans 8:28).*

**Reflect on the following and then use the space provided to journal your thoughts.**

- *Locate yourself in the reading. What thoughts and feelings immediately come to mind?*
- *Did the passage of scripture help or challenge you in any way?*
- *Were you able to recognize the extension of God's love in this reading?*
- *What do you take away from the reading? How will you apply what you've read?*
- *What will you share with others?*

# A Place for Your Thoughts (Now ...)
## Searching

Date: _____

# A Place for Your Thoughts (Sometime later ...)
## Searching

Date:

# SURRENDER

*Death and life are in the power of the tongue, and those who love it will eat its fruit (Proverbs 18:21 NKJV).*

Have you noticed that our tongues, the smallest organ in our bodies, can wield great power and influence oftentimes without permission? And before we know it, a barrage of negative words begin spewing out of our mouths. It takes a few moments for our minds to catch up to what is happening, but by that point, it is too late. The insults have already happened, people have been offended, deals have been made, and doors have been opened for the enemy to enter our situations.

What happened? Our tongues got away from us and went in a direction of their own, *Even so the tongue is a little member, and boasteth great things. Behold, how great a matter a little fire kindleth! And the tongue is a fire, a world of iniquity: so is the tongue among our members, that it defileth the whole body, and setteth on fire the course of nature; and it is set on fire of hell (James 3:5-6).* Who would think that such a small thing could cause such an uproar and carry such power?

Every tongue, especially the tongue of the believer, with all its power, authority, and influence, is required to make a full surrender of itself to the Lord. The surrender is necessary as the tongue can be filled with grace and mercy one day and be full of cursing, deceit, and fraud the next. Job knew the imperativeness of bringing his tongue under submission when he stated, *My lips shall not speak wickedness, nor my tongue utter deceit (Job 27:4).* The writer of Proverbs stated, *A wholesome tongue is a tree of life: but perverseness therein is a breach in the spirit (Proverbs 15:4).*

Surrendering, saying yes when you really want to say no, can be terrifying. However, it is imperative that we control our tongues. Proverbs 6:2 gives this warning, *Thou art snared with the words of thy mouth, thou art taken with the words of thy mouth.* Regrettably, I have been taken and snared by the words of my mouth many times over the years, which has cost me many good relationships. If we desire the character of Christ, then we must practice these principles. *For he that will love life, and see good days, let him refrain his tongue from evil, and his lips that they speak no guile (1 Peter 3:10),* and *Let your speech be always with grace, seasoned with salt, that ye may know how ye ought to answer every man (Colossians 4:6).*

Should you find yourself ensnared or taken by your words in a situation, *Do this now, my son, and deliver thyself, when thou art come into the hand of thy friend; go, humble thyself, and make sure thy friend (Proverbs 6:3)*. The love of God will cover you. Let us use wisdom in carefully choosing the words that we speak, especially when we arise in the early morning. Our words of submission (or the lack thereof) set the tone for our day. It usually holds true that if the first fruits of our morning are holy, our entire day will be holy.

**Reflect on the following and then use the space provided to journal your thoughts.**

- *Locate yourself in the reading. What thoughts and feelings immediately come to mind?*
- *Did the passage of scripture help or challenge you in any way?*
- *Were you able to recognize the extension of God's love in this reading?*
- *What do you take away from the reading? How will you apply what you've read?*
- *What will you share with others?*

# A Place for Your Thoughts (Now ...)
## Surrender

Date:

# A Place for Your Thoughts (Sometime later ...)
## Surrender

Date:

# THE GAME CHANGER

*For whom he did foreknow, he also did predestinate to be conformed to the image of his Son (Romans 8:29).*

On several occasions, when I entered a room, immediately, the talking and laughter stopped, and people turned their eyes upon me. Others ceased from doing things that appeared to be unseemly and began making attempts to correct themselves. It is always most interesting to see. I have learned to smile and to greet everyone graciously, knowing that it is the Christ in me that has now changed the atmosphere. His abiding presence in the life of the believer is a game-changer and a course corrector. When any of His children displaying His righteous image occupy a space or walk into a room; all bets are off. Whatever the enemy had in His mind is now in jeopardy! We have the power to command righteousness and to bring light into any situation and in any place at any time because of His presence in us. We bring Him! When we show up in His image with His power, the game changes. We have no power of our own, but we have been given power by the license and authority of the Holy Ghost. We are game changers!

The Lord has not called us to be status quo, run of the mill Christians. Nor has He required certain degrees of education, superior intelligence, or financial affluence in order to be a game changer. In fact, Titus 2:14 refers to us as peculiar people. Matthew 5:13 says we are the salt of the earth, and 1 Peter 2:9 declares us a chosen generation, a royal priesthood, and a holy nation. None of this sounds "regular" to me. It is the irregular people, those who choose to be exempt from the world's standards, who are most effective in bringing about change. Paul, the Apostle (a real game changer), summed it up this way. *For ye see your calling, brethren, how that not many wise men after the flesh, not many mighty, not many noble, are called: But God hath chosen the foolish things of the world to confound the wise, and God hath chosen the weak things of the world to confound the things which are mighty; And base things of the world, and things which are despised, hath God chosen, yea, and things which are not, to bring to nought things that are (1 Corinthians 1:26-28).*

Christ, the Game Changer, is in you! So, go ahead, don't be scared! Be the game changer God has designed you to be! Others are counting on you to make a difference in their lives.

**Reflect on the following and then use the space provided to journal your thoughts.**

- *Locate yourself in the reading. What thoughts and feelings immediately come to mind?*
- *Did the passage of scripture help or challenge you in any way?*
- *Were you able to recognize the extension of God's love in this reading?*
- *What do you take away from the reading? How will you apply what you've read?*
- *What will you share with others?*

# A Place for Your Thoughts (Now ...)
## Game Changer

Date: _____

# A Place for Your Thoughts (Sometime later ...)
## Game Changer

Date:

# THE REAL ENEMY

*For we wrestle not against flesh and blood, but against principalities, against powers, against the rulers of the darkness of this world, against spiritual wickedness in high places (Ephesians 6:12).*

How often do we say, "It's all your fault," or "I had no choice, they made me do it?" As humans, it is in our nature to focus on other people as the source of our irritation and the creators of our problems. Therefore, logic says that we must wage warfare against them to stand our ground, to be vindicated, and to become victorious overcomers. However, this thinking is far from the truth.

The truth is when we blame people for our misfortune, our warfare is ineffective. Our warfare is with the principalities, powers, and the rulers of darkness in high places that influence and drive the behaviors of people who have been overpowered by spiritual wickedness as addressed in 1 Peter 5:8. *Be sober, be vigilant; because your adversary the devil, as a roaring lion, walketh about, seeking whom he may devour.* We cannot expect to engage in battle with spiritual entities without the help and intervention of God. We would surely be defeated but, *Our God will fight for us (Nehemiah 4:20 NKJV).*

It is the resistance that we struggle with, resistance in submitting our will to God's will and our ways to God's ways. Resistance makes us prey to the influence of the roaring lion, just as our brethren whom we blame as the source of our problems. If this is so, where then lies our victory? It lies in James 4:6-7. *Wherefore he saith, God resisteth the proud, but giveth grace unto the humble. Submit yourselves therefore to God. Resist the devil, and he will flee from you.*

That being said, our battle then belongs to the Lord, who is well able to handle every situation and defeat every foe. Psalm 89:23 gives us this assurance, *And I will beat down his foes before his face, and plague them that hate him.* This place of submission is also where we see the effectiveness of the spiritual armor given us. *Wherefore take unto you the whole armour of God, that ye may be able to withstand in the evil day, and having done all, to stand. Stand therefore, having your loins girt about with truth, and having on the breastplate of righteousness; And your feet shod with the preparation of the gospel of peace; Above all, taking the shield of faith, wherewith ye shall be able to quench all the fiery darts of the wicked. And take the helmet of salvation, and the sword of the Spirit, which is the word of God (Ephesians 6:13-18).*

Obedient submission is also the catalyst that ignites our weapons of prayer, worship, and fasting. They are a source of continual strength as we take our eyes off of people and fix our gaze upon Christ, who fights for us and is the source of true victory. *But thanks be to God, which giveth us the victory through our Lord Jesus Christ (1 Corinthians 15:57).*

**Reflect on the following and then use the space provided to journal your thoughts.**
- *Locate yourself in the reading. What thoughts and feelings immediately come to mind?*
- *Did the passage of scripture help or challenge you in any way?*
- *Were you able to recognize the extension of God's love in this reading?*
- *What do you take away from the reading? How will you apply what you've read?*
- *What will you share with others?*

# A Place for Your Thoughts (Now ...)
## The Real Enemy

Date:

# A Place for Your Thoughts (Sometime later ...)
## The Real Enemy

Date:

# GOD'S LOVE THINKS HIGHER

*For as the heavens are higher than the earth, so are my ways higher than your ways, and my thoughts than your thoughts (Isaiah 55:9).*

Just when we think we have it all figured out, the dots connected, and all the pieces in the right places, we discover that our picture does not look like His. As much as we confess that we have the mind of Christ, we will never have the complete picture, *But as it is written, Eye hath not seen, nor ear heard, neither have entered into the heart of man, the things which God hath prepared for them that love him (1 Corinthians 2:9).* God's thoughts are far beyond ours. His ways are undiscoverable. We are clueless, unless He opens our eyes to a glimpse of His vision.

Yes, we have thoughts and ideas that come to us from the Lord. This is where most problems occur. Rather than submitting those given thoughts and ideas back to the Lord for further guidance and instruction, we go about doing things our way. It is like saying to God, "Great idea, I will take it from here." In our zeal and enthusiasm, we often forget Proverbs 3:5-6, *Trust in the LORD with all thine heart; and lean not unto thine own understanding. In all thy ways acknowledge him, and he shall direct thy paths.* Verse seven follows, *Be not wise in thine own eyes.* We need this restraint because He sees the bigger picture. While we are busy focusing on the benefits and blessings, the Lord is trying to navigate us through the problems and the pitfalls.

What then shall we do with the thoughts and ideas given us from the Lord? We wait and position ourselves to hear a further word from Him. Every step we take must come as a directive from the Holy Spirit. *And thine ears shall hear a word behind thee, saying, This is the way, walk ye in it, when ye turn to the right hand, and when ye turn to the left (Isaiah 30:21).* Wait on the Lord.

**Reflect on the following and then use the space provided to journal your thoughts.**

- *Locate yourself in the reading. What thoughts and feelings immediately come to mind?*
- *Did the passage of scripture help or challenge you in any way?*
- *Were you able to recognize the extension of God's love in this reading?*
- *What do you take away from the reading? How will you apply what you've read?*
- *What will you share with others?*

# A Place for Your Thoughts (Now ...)
## Think Higher

Date:

# A Place for Your Thoughts (Sometime later …)
## Think Higher

Date:

# GOD'S LOVE IS TRUTH

*God is a Spirit: and they that worship him must worship him in spirit and in truth (John 4:24).*

God is a man of truth, and His Word always speaks truth. Therefore, to worship God effectively, we must operate in the same manner, by speaking truth and allowing it to govern every decision. Should there be a question regarding His truth, we have the Bible, the written Word of God for confirmation and clarification. 2 Timothy 3:16 states, *All scripture is given by inspiration of God, and is profitable for doctrine, for reproof, for correction, for instruction in righteousness.*

Understanding scripture can be quite challenging. Its teachings are not always comfortable or welcomed. When the Word of Truth is received in the heart and acted upon, it is worship to God. And truth spoken in love through the believer becomes a comfort to the comfortless and water to the thirsty soul. Truth is also a discerner of the thoughts and intents of man's heart. Many lies and deceptive plans have been uncovered by a simple word of truth. Wisdom comes in understanding the liberating power of truth. *And ye shall know the truth, and the truth shall make you free (John 8:32).*

**Reflect on the following and then use the space provided to journal your thoughts.**

- *Locate yourself in the reading. What thoughts and feelings immediately come to mind?*
- *Did the passage of scripture help or challenge you in any way?*
- *Were you able to recognize the extension of God's love in this reading?*
- *What do you take away from the reading? How will you apply what you've read?*
- *What will you share with others?*

# A Place for Your Thoughts (Now ...)
## Truth

Date:

# A Place for Your Thoughts (Sometime later ...)
## Truth

Date:

# GOD'S LOVE LAUGHS

*He that sitteth in the heavens shall laugh: the Lord shall have them in derision (Psalm 2:4).*

The Lord rejoices with us in every victory and triumph of life. The Lord's laughter and delight can be heard in the heavens, *He that sitteth in the heavens shall laugh: the Lord shall have them in derision (Psalm 2:4).*

"Push 'em back, push 'em back, way back," was a cheer heard at high school football games as the offensive team advanced towards the defense. The goal was to stop the advancement, push them back, and score a win. As Christians, our goal is to stop the advancement of the enemy. We can learn from the example of Jesus when He was in the wilderness being tempted by the devil in Matthew 4. Each time Jesus responded to the enemy with the Word of God, he was pushed back. *But he answered and said, It is written, Man shall not live by bread alone, but by every word that proceedeth out of the mouth of God (Matthew 4:4).* **Push back!** *Jesus said unto him, It is written again, Thou shalt not tempt the Lord thy God (Matthew 4:7).* **Push back!** *Then saith Jesus unto him, Get thee hence, Satan: for it is written, Thou shalt worship the Lord thy God, and him only shalt thou serve (Matthew 4:10).* **Push back!** Finally, we read in Matthew 4:11; *Then the devil leaveth him.* **Touch down!**

In Christ, we are strong. Through His Word, we have the power and ability to push back when attacked. There may be times in the midst of the battle when we may have to encourage ourselves as others have done. *And David was greatly distressed; for the people spake of stoning him, ... but David encouraged himself in the Lord his God (1 Samuel 30:6).* Be courageous in every situation and **push back!**

With every **push back**, the Lord laughs!

**Reflect on the following and then use the space provided to journal your thoughts.**

- *Locate yourself in the reading. What thoughts and feelings immediately come to mind?*
- *Did the passage of scripture help or challenge you in any way?*
- *Were you able to recognize the extension of God's love in this reading?*
- *What do you take away from the reading? How will you apply what you've read?*
- *What will you share with others?*

# A Place for Your Thoughts (Now ...)
## Laughs

Date: _____

# A Place for Your Thoughts (Sometime later ...)
## Laughs

Date:

# GOD'S LOVE IS WATCHFUL

*For I am jealous over you with godly jealously*
*(2 Corinthians 11:2).*

The love of God watches over us with an intense jealousy. In John 17:11, Jesus prayed, *Holy Father, keep through thine own name those whom thou hast given me, that they may be one, as we are.* The Father has given us to His Son, our Bridegroom for safe keeping. We have this guarantee in John 6:39, *that of all which he hath given me I should lose nothing, but should raise it up again at the last day.* Every good bridegroom watches for and cares for His bride, keeping her from the roving eyes of wolves that come to steal, to kill, and to destroy.

*In my Father's house are many mansions: if it were not so, I would have told you. I go to prepare a place for you. And if I go and prepare a place for you, I will come again, and receive you unto myself; that where I am, there ye may be also (John 14:2-3).* Jesus has prepared a place for His bride where there are no wolves, and the enemy cannot break through and steal. In the meantime, His watchful eye oversees our journey through the pitfalls of life, removing debris from our way as long as we remain in His care and on His path. Should we find ourselves plagued with situations and harmful adversities, perhaps we have taken ourselves out of the His protective hands. If so, let us retrace our steps and get back on the right road.

We await with anticipation of that glorious day when we will rejoice with Him at the Marriage Supper of the Lamb. We dare not miss it as the door will open at an hour unexpected. *And at midnight there was a cry made, Behold, the bridegroom cometh; go ye out to meet him (Matthew 25:6).* The wise are prepared and remain under His watchful eye. The foolish, who take themselves from under the watchful hand of the Father, may miss the opening. The question for them then becomes, "When will the door open again?"

*Seek ye the Lord while he may be found, call ye upon him while he is near: Let the wicked forsake his way, and the unrighteous man his thoughts: and let him return unto the Lord, and he will have mercy upon him; and to our God, for he will abundantly pardon (Isaiah 55:6-7).*

**Reflect on the following and then use the space provided to journal your thoughts.**

- *Locate yourself in the reading. What thoughts and feelings immediately come to mind?*
- *Did the passage of scripture help or challenge you in any way?*
- *Were you able to recognize the extension of God's love in this reading?*
- *What do you take away from the reading? How will you apply what you've read?*
- *What will you share with others?*

# A Place for Your Thoughts (Now ...)
## Watchful

Date:

# A Place for Your Thoughts (Sometime later ...)
## Watchful

Date:

# WHAT SHALL I DO?

*If any of you lack wisdom, let him ask of God, that giveth to all men liberally, and upbraideth not; and it shall be given him (James 1:5).*

Ever asked the question, what shall I do? Wouldn't it be nice to have a universal answer to this question, one that is effective and applicable to every situation we face in this life? I believe the key to getting an answer depends on whom you are asking the question. If you are asking friends, family, and the peanut gallery, your answers will vary according to their circumstances, their emotions, and mode of thinking at the time. If you are asking of the Lord, the answer will remain the same just as He is the same yesterday, today, and forever (Hebrews 13:8).

So, I chose to ask the question of the Lord, and in His fashion, He responded right away, giving me a two-part answer that can be applied in any given situation. Part one, "you shall remain at peace" according to John 14:27. *Peace I leave with you, my peace I give unto you: not as the world giveth, give I unto you. Let not your heart be troubled, neither let it be afraid.* God will release His supernatural peace into our hearts, which can override any unrest the world has to offer. Part 2, "Be *ye steadfast, unmovable, always abounding in the work of the Lord" (1 Corinthians 15:58).* He went on to say, remain steady, and in your stability, rescue others as you would rescue someone from a fire, have mercy on everyone who needs it, and abstain from every appearance of evil.

I was given the choice to accept or reject His answer. I chose to accept His answer, especially since it was the only one offered. In my mind, I was looking for something more specific and detailed to the situation. But I soon came to realize that His peace automatically brings specificity and that remaining steady within the context of His Word and promises, keeps us grounded in truth. With truth comes freedom, *And ye shall know the truth, and the truth shall make you free (John 8:32).*

I trust His answers, which are always right. He is not a liar. You too can have this same assurance if you choose to accept and act upon God's universal answer to the question, "What shall I do." Not only will you always have an answer for yourself, but one that will work for others as well.

**Reflect on the following and then use the space provided to journal your thoughts.**

- *Locate yourself in the reading. What thoughts and feelings immediately come to mind?*
- *Did the passage of scripture help or challenge you in any way?*
- *Were you able to recognize the extension of God's love in this reading?*
- *What do you take away from the reading? How will you apply what you've read?*
- *What will you share with others?*

# A Place for Your Thoughts (Now ...)
## Wisdom

Date:

# A Place for Your Thoughts (Sometime later ...)
## Wisdom

Date:

# YOU ARE THE ONE

*For many are called, but few are chosen*
*(Matthew 22:14).*

Years ago, I heard a pastor make the statement, "You are the one." I heard it as more than just a statement; it was an emphatic declaration, "You are the one!" I stopped in my tracks, realizing I am the one! Instantly, my struggle came to an end.

I struggled with doubts and questions just as many others do. Had God really called me to do something for Him? Was I the one He placed His spirit in and anointing on? And was I the one He would use to bless many lives? In my heart, I knew indeed that I was the one. The picture was clear, and the evidence was manifested. Yet, my mind still struggled with that assurance. The threads of deception too fine to recognize weaved with the opinions of others, religious tradition, and jealousy often undermined my confidence. But on this day, the light bulb came on, exposing the threads and freeing me from the cobwebs of doubt. I had indeed been called by God to be the one.

I thought of Stephen, a man among the crowds of people chosen by God for a unique position. *Wherefore, brethren, look ye out among you seven men of honest report, full of the Holy Ghost and wisdom, whom we may appoint over this business (Acts 6:3).* He was appointed to distribute food to the widows and to serve tables. His food ministry quickly evolved into much more, *And Stephen, full of faith and power, did great wonders and miracles among the people (Acts 6:8).* He was chosen to help move the apostle's ministry forward, chosen to work among the people, and chosen to stir up the stony hearts of the Pharisees, drawing them out of their complacency. He was the one chosen to be the first martyr to die for the cause of Christ. He was also the one for whom Jesus stood up from His seat in Heaven, *But he, being full of the Holy Ghost, looked up steadfastly into heaven, and saw the glory of God, and Jesus standing on the right hand of God (Acts 7:55).* He was the one.

Just as Stephen, each of us are called to be the one from the foundation of the world. All of God's children are blessed and equipped with specific gifts and talents that make us the one. We are not an oops, nor an after-thought. We are the ones He will use to touch and to minister to the hearts of others. We are hope givers, peacemakers, and the embodiment of Christ extending the fruits of His character to the world.

161 | *God's Love Poured Out*

You and I are the ones. We have been uniquely made and fashioned by His hand for a specific purpose that only we can fulfill. You are the One!

*Ye have not chosen me, but I have chosen you, and ordained you, that ye should go and bring forth fruit, and that your fruit should remain (John 15:16).*

**Reflect on the following and then use the space provided to journal your thoughts.**

- *Locate yourself in the reading. What thoughts and feelings immediately come to mind?*
- *Did the passage of scripture help or challenge you in any way?*
- *Were you able to recognize the extension of God's love in this reading?*
- *What do you take away from the reading? How will you apply what you've read?*
- *What will you share with others?*

# A Place for Your Thoughts (Now ...)
## You Are the One

Date:

# A Place for Your Thoughts (Sometime later ...)
## You Are the One

Date:

# YOUR CHOICE

*He that believeth on the Son hath everlasting life: and he that believeth not the Son shall not see life; but the wrath of God abideth on him (John 3:36).*

What will you lose by believing that Jesus is the Son of God? What will you lose by believing in the eternal life that He offers? What will you lose in opening your heart and asking Christ to forgive your sins and to fill your life with His presence?

If you indeed believe that Jesus Christ is the Son of God, you will have lost nothing, but you will have gained eternal salvation. If you believe that Jesus died for your sins and has prepared a place in Heaven for you at the end of this natural life, you will have lost nothing, but you will have gained a permanent home with the King of Kings and the Lord of Lords.

So, what will you lose? Will you lose your status among those who despise the thought of Christ being the Messiah? Will you lose friendship with those who say that there is no God? Will you lose having your name written in The Book of Life? (Revelation 20:15) Will you lose your permanent place in the lake of fire with that old dragon called the Devil, Satan, the false prophet, and the beast? What will you lose?

Our choices are governed by what we believe to be true and by what we say. Jesus says, *I the LORD search the heart, I try the reins, even to give every man according to his ways, and according to the fruit of his doings (Jeremiah 17:10).* It is our choice, *I call heaven and earth to record this day against you, that I have set before you life and death, blessing and cursing: therefore choose life, that both thou and thy seed may live (Deuteronomy 30:19).*

What will you choose?

**Reflect on the following and then use the space provided to journal your thoughts.**

- *Locate yourself in the reading. What thoughts and feelings immediately come to mind?*
- *Did the passage of scripture help or challenge you in any way?*
- *Were you able to recognize the extension of God's love in this reading?*
- *What do you take away from the reading? How will you apply what you've read?*
- *What will you share with others?*

# A Place for Your Thoughts (Now ...)
## Choices

Date: _____

# A Place for Your Thoughts (Sometime later ...)
## Choices

Date:

## ABOUT THE AUTHOR

Darlene Palmer found, in Jesus, the peace that surpasses all understanding when she gave her life to Christ in April of 1980. Her service to the Lord has spanned 40 years, during which she has served in all aspects of ministry receiving her ministerial license in October of 1998. She retired from thirteen plus years of working in the non-profit sector, servicing the community as a case manager for homeless women and their children. She remains a mentor to many.

A native of Southern California, Darlene graduated from Bible college earning a Bachelor of Ministry degree from Vision International University.

When she isn't hosting seminars and retreats, the mother of four prefers to spend time with her children and enjoying the presence of the Lord.

www.ingramcontent.com/pod-product-compliance
Ingram Content Group UK Ltd.
Pitfield, Milton Keynes, MK11 3LW, UK
UKHW051302180426
11947UKWH00020B/1862